WALKS AROUND LANCASTER

10 WALKS UNDER 7 MILES

Dalesman

First published in 2006 by Dalesman
an imprint of
Country Publications Ltd
The Water Mill
Broughton Hall
Skipton
North Yorkshire BD23 3AG

Reprinted 2009

Text © Terry Marsh 2006
Maps © Gelder Design & Mapping 2006
Illustrations © Christine Isherwood 2006

Cover: Crook o' Lune by Jon Sparks

A British Library Cataloguing-in-Publication record
is available for this book

ISBN 978-1-85568-230-6

Printed by Amadeus Press

PUBLISHER'S NOTE
The information given in this book has been provided in good faith and is intended only
as a general guide. Whilst all reasonable efforts have been made to ensure that details
were correct at the time of publication, the author and Country Publications Ltd
cannot accept any responsibility for inaccuracies. It is the responsibility of individuals
undertaking outdoor activities to approach the activity with caution and, especially if
inexperienced, to do so under appropriate supervision. The activity described in this book
is strenuous and individuals should ensure that they are suitably fit before embarking
upon it. They should carry the appropriate equipment and maps, be properly clothed and
have adequate footwear. They should also take note of weather conditions and forecasts,
and leave notice of their intended route and estimated time of return.

Contents

Walk 1
Clougha Pike   4¼ miles (7 km)   5

Walk 2
Crook o' Lune   3¾ miles (6 km)   8

Walk 3
Morecambe Bay   4¼ miles (7 km)   10

Walk 4
Annas Ghyll   4 miles (6.5 km)   12

Walk 5
Lancaster and Slyne   6¼ miles (10 km)   15

Walk 6
Glasson Dock   6½ miles (10.5 km)   18

Walk 7
Galgate and Thurnham   5¼ miles (8.5 km)   21

Walk 8
Lancaster: city and canal   7 miles (11 km)   24

Walk 9
Littledale   5 miles (8 km)   27

Walk 10
Carnforth and the Keer   6¼ miles (10 km)   30

Introduction

Lancaster is an important, ancient and hugely historic city in the story of the County Palatine of Lancashire. And even though the administrative centre of the county is not in Lancaster (it's in Preston), very few Lancastrians regard this city as other than the historical capital. What isn't immediately obvious is that the city is a great focal point for walks. Its position on the River Lune enables riverside walks, while the beautiful Lancaster Canal, originally planned to run from Kendal to Wigan, passes right through the heart of the city, and lets you set off north or south.

The walks in this book reach from Carnforth in the north, a modest town made eternally famous by the fact that the 1945 film *Brief Encounter*, starring Trevor Howard and Celia Johnson, was filmed at Carnforth railway station, something of a poignant spot for film buffs. The station café is newly refurbished in the style of the 1940s. In the south, it is impossible to ignore the lovely coastal scenery south of Glasson Dock and around to Cockersand Abbey, these days something of a forlorn edifice overlooking Morecambe Bay.

Inland, the River Lune provides the excuse for an easy walk into a scene famously painted by Turner, and much enjoyed by the poet Thomas Gray. And there's a chance to explore some of the hidden dales and villages of Lancashire, like Brookhouse, Galgate, Slyne and the remote Littledale.

The proximity of many of the walks to the coastal waters means that the walks in this book often lead across countryside that is also a habitat for a wide range of birds. So, taking a pair of binoculars is always a good idea. It's also often breezy, too, so something warm to wear is vital.

None of the walks in this book is excessively demanding, but you should approach them with caution if you are inexperienced. Always wear boots and appropriate clothing, and carry the relevant Ordnance Survey map.

Clougha Pike

> **Distance:** 4¼ miles (7 km)
> **Time:** 2½-3 hours
> **Terrain:** Good paths and upland tracks; one short trackless section
> **Start/Finish:** Birk Bank car park, Rigg Lane, Quernmore, grid ref 526604
> **Map:** Explorer OL41 (Forest of Bowland & Ribblesdale)

A lovely walk best reserved for a clear day when the views northwards reach over Lancaster and the coast to the distant frieze of Lakeland fells and the high Pennine mountains. Although much of the walk is on access land, dogs are not permitted.

Set off through a nearby gate onto a broad track through bracken, and, when it forks, branch left. When the track later bends right, leave it by bearing left onto a narrower path that continues easily to Ottergear Bridge, spanning a gully near a disused quarry. Over the bridge, bear left on a broad track that leads to a T-junction. Here, turn right. Climb gently for a short distance and then level out as the track goes through a gully. Cross a ladder-stile. Climb steeply out of the gully onto a constructed track that rises steadily onto the moorland above.

The track offers a splendid range of views that improve with every step. Follow this for just over a mile (2 km) to its highest point near a small quarry area. Now abandon the

Snipe inhabit moorland and marshy ground. The long, straight bill makes them instantly recognisable.

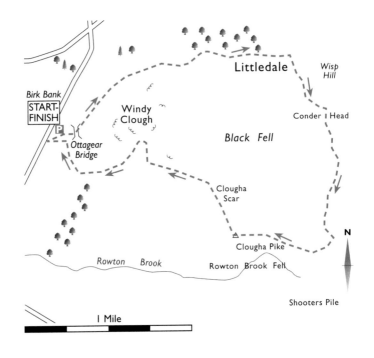

track for untracked ground by stepping into the adjacent heather. Head in a roughly south-west direction to locate and cross a low step-stile in a fence, about 300 yards from the summit of Clougha Pike. There are plenty of gritstone boulders to ease progress, but the choice of route is entirely your own.

Once over the stile, bear right on a clear path to the top of Clougha Pike, which is marked by a trig pillar and a stone shelter. On most days you can see the Lakeland Fells and the Three Peaks of Yorkshire, and sometimes the Isle of Man and the Clwydian Hills in North Wales.

Heading roughly north, leave Clougha Pike by following a peaty path punctuated by gritstone that roughly follows the edge of a low escarpment on the left, and aims first for a large cairn. Then descend, again on a clear path, with a fenceline gradually converging from the right.

Where the fence and wall meet, bear left down a short rock step. Follow the wall for about 400 yards until it reaches a more level stretch. Here, keep an eye open for a path branching left (ignore the ladder-stile ahead). Go down through scattered boulders, then descend across a rough pasture to a gate in a wall corner.

Through the gate bear right through reeds, still descending. The path threads a way round to Windy Clough, an obvious gash through the descending ridge on your right. At the edge of Windy Clough, go left to a ladder-stile. Descend through a shallow gully flanked by bilberries and bracken. The path is often overgrown, but it's easy enough to follow, going through light woodland. Later the path accompanies a stream, and passes through an area of gorse and on to a stretch of boardwalks around the edge of a marshy area that is filled in spring with rafts of bog cotton and bog asphodel.

The path soon meets a track beside a gate. Turn right. When it forks a short way further on, bear left over a slight rise to a track junction. Go left again to descend to the car park.

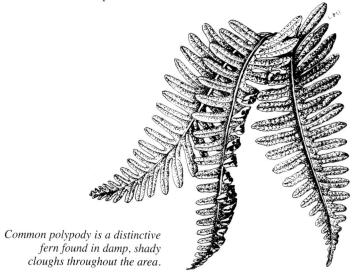

Common polypody is a distinctive fern found in damp, shady cloughs throughout the area.

Crook o' Lune and Caton

Distance: 3³/₄ miles (6 km)
Time: 2 hours
Terrain: Riverside paths and old railway trackbed
Start/Finish: Crook o' Lune car park, grid ref 521648
Map: Explorer OL41 (Forest of Bowland & Ribblesdale)

This is a lovely and very easy walk beside the River Lune with excellent chances of seeing a wide range of birdlife, especially in summer when the sand martins return.

Set off from the car park by passing through a gate to the left of the artwork depicting the scene of Turner's renowned painting of this spot. Descend to meet the riverbank. Simply follow it easily, keeping an eye open for birds on the river and in the meadows, until you reach the large and obvious structure of an aqueduct.

Cross this, and step-stiles on the other side. Turn left, now on the true left bank of the river. Follow the course of the river as it sweeps round, with Ingleborough, one of Yorkshire's Three Peaks, in the far distance. After passing through a gate, the riverside path becomes a wide stony track that soon moves away from the river, heading towards the village of Caton.

Sand martins are a common sight along the River Lune between March and October.

8

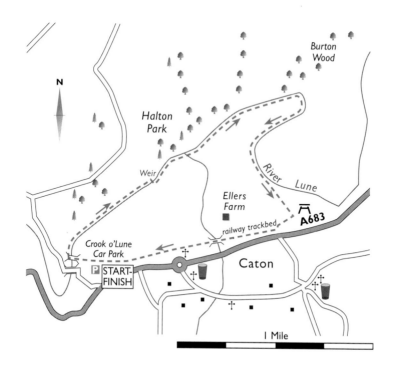

Just before reaching the main road, turn right onto an old railway trackbed, formerly a stretch of the Lancaster to Wennington railway line, now part of the River Lune Millennium Park. When the trackbed reaches a surfaced lane, keep forward (Caton lies just to the left if you want to go in search of refreshment).

Keep ahead along the trackbed, which will guide you back to the start at Crook o' Lune.

Walkers wanting to make a little more of this walk can begin at Skerton Bridge in Lancaster, and follow a surfaced path alongside the river, heading out of the city. This eventually passes beneath the M6 motorway and passes the village of Halton on the opposite side of the river, and continues quite delightfully all the way to Crook o' Lune. Of course, you'll need to retrace this section on the way back, but it's such an agreeable stretch, with the occasionally turbulent Lune for company, that it really is no hardship to do so. Altogether it will double the walk.

Morecambe Bay

Distance: 4¼ miles (7 km)
Time: 2 hours
Terrain: canal walking; good paths; some muddy
foreshore walking
Start/Finish: Hest Bank foreshore car park, grid ref 468666
Map: Explorers 296 (Lancaster, Morecambe & Fleetwood)

An often breezy start along the foreshore of Morecambe Bay introduces a lovely, peaceful return along a stretch of the Lancaster Canal.

Start by walking along the lane across the foreshore at Hest Bank, and soon pass the entrance to a caravan site. When the on-going track forks, branch left onto the foreshore itself and walk to a car park near Morecambe Lodge.

Here, abandon the foreshore for a while. Go across the parking area, and onto a broad track. Cross to a stile near a gate. Walk up the middle of a field, gradually moving to the left to locate a step-stile in a corner. Now go ahead along a field edge, and descend to a stile near Red Bank Farm caravan site.

Over the stile go through the farmyard, and out onto a surfaced lane, which parallels a raised embankment. At the end of the lane, keep following the embankment. Finally descend steps and stride along a path leading out to meet another lane. Turn left here, and shortly go right to pass in front of Wild Duck Hall.

Follow the lane (St Nicholas Lane) up towards housing at the edge of Bolton-le-Sands. Finally bear right, walking the wrong way down a one-way street, to meet the A6.

Shelduck favour coastal habitats such as the mudflats of Morecambe Bay.

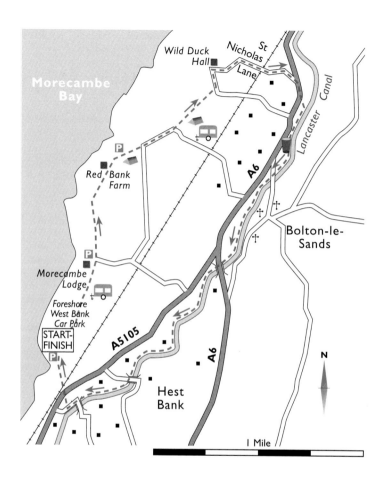

Cross slightly to the right to enter a lane that leads up to the Lancaster Canal, joining the canal towpath. Turn right.

Eventually leave the towpath by walking up a ramp at Bridge 118 to a road. Go down the road and take the first turning on the right (Station Road). Descend to meet the A6 once more.

Cross with care, and head for the railway crossing. Over the crossing, bear right onto a surfaced track to complete the walk.

Annas Ghyll

Distance: 4 miles (6.5 km)
Time: 2 hours
Terrain: variable field paths and farm tracks; some road walking
Start/Finish: Bull Beck Picnic Site and Car Park, Caton,
grid ref 541649
Map: Explorer OL41 (Forest of Bowland & Ribblesdale)

This is a quiet and agreeable walk mainly across open country, using ancient trackways and visiting the site of an old mill before returning through the lovely village of Brookhouse.

Leave the Bull Beck car park and return to the Lancaster to Hornby road. Walk east, away from Caton, but only for about 200 yards. Then, as the road bends to the left, leave it by crossing a step-stile on the right, beside a gate. Walk up the field to a mid-field waymark. Now continue to an obsolete step-stile at an old field boundary. Now head across to the far top corner of the field. A metal kissing-gate gives onto a narrow path leading out to an estate road (Kirk Beck Close) on the edge of Brookhouse. Turn left to a T-junction, and go left again. After about 400 yards, and on reaching the last house, leave the road over a step-stile on the right.

Now walk up an old sunken track flanked rather sparsely with tired old hawthorns, an aged oak and a solitary ash. The track climbs gently. From the high point, with some lovely views, you continue in the same direction, still following the course of the old track, though it is a little less obvious now. Head for a stile through a wall. From it, go forward along the left-hand field boundary. When this changes direction, maintain the same direction as you go down a sloping pasture to a wall corner.

From the corner, walk on, with the wall on your right, to a narrow stone stile, beyond which you go on to reach Annas Ghyll Farm.

On reaching the farm, pass through a gate. Immediately swing right to cross a cattle grid, and start up the farm access track. At the highest point of the track, a couple of log benches offer a breather and a fine view of the Lune

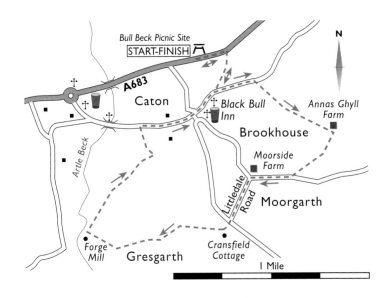

Valley. Continue by crossing another cattle grid. Carry on along the farm access eventually to meet a country lane.

Turn right, descending gently to a road junction with a small post box opposite. Turn left (Littledale Road). Walk up to another road junction, and there cross into the driveway leading up to Cransfield Cottage. On reaching the first buildings, turn to the right of them to a step-stile (waymarked for the Caton Village Walk). Go forward along a broad, sunken track, usually flooded. Follow this as it swings right to a stile below an overhead powerline. From this, keep on in much the same direction, to pass through a collapsed wall just to the right of an ash tree. Keep on to reach the remains of another wall, which contains some upright slabs called vaccary stones, indicative of ancient farmland, a 'vaccary' being a medieval farmstead.

Cross another step-stile. Go forward along the left-hand edge of a field to a ladder-stile. Over this, bear half-right across the ensuing pasture towards a solitary tree, and a wall. Walk alongside the wall to another ladder-stile, near a wall corner. Over the stile, go forward across the corner of a sloping pasture. Descend beside first a fence and later a wall.

The wall guides you down to a step-stile at the head of a walled track. Go down this to the site of Forge Mill. At the bottom of the track you meet a surfaced lane above Artle Beck. Turn right, following the lane for 300 yards

to a group of farm buildings on the left. Leave the lane by crossing a step-stile on the right. Go on in the same direction across a paddock to locate a signpost in a fence corner. Here, pass through a metal kissing-gate, and continue with a hedge on your left. Cross another stile and keep on in the same direction along a line of mature hawthorn interspersed with holly. Do the same in the next field to reach another corner stile.

Keep on beside a fence and hedge. Eventually, at the rear of houses, you reach a short, boarded section leading to a kissing-gate giving on to an enclosed path between houses. You emerge into a housing estate. Keep left for a short distance. As the estate road swings right, go forward down another enclosed path. At the end of this, turn right along the main village road.

The distinctive oak is our commonest deciduous tree.

Go past the Black Bull Inn and the parish church, and into Caton Green Road. Turn left into Kirk Beck Close, and then right along the signposted, narrow path used earlier in the walk. From the kissing-gate, go across the field to that obsolete step-stile. Bear left down to the valley road, retracing your steps to the car park.

Lancaster and Slyne

Distance: 6¹/₄ miles (10 km)
Time: 3 hours
Terrain: canal walking, trackless fields, some road walking
Start/Finish: Riverside Park car park, Lancaster, grid ref 480624
Map: Explorer OL41 (Forest of Bowland & Ribblesdale)

With the intention of making the most of the lovely Lancaster Canal, this walk first heads across country to the village of Slyne, before joining the canal towpath for easy walking back to Lancaster. Keep an eye open along the canal banks for kingfisher.

Leave the car park and turn right along the surfaced path alongside the River Lune, part of the Millennium Park that makes use of an old railway trackbed. Follow this until you reach the large and obvious structure of the Lune Aqueduct, which carries the Lancaster Canal across the river. From the base of the aqueduct, a flight of steps leads up to the canal towpath. Here, turn left and cross the aqueduct. On the other side, walk on to the first bridge (no 108).

Just on reaching the bridge, turn left up to the road. Cross the bridge, then immediately go left down to a step-stile. Follow the edge of the field to another stile in a corner, beyond which you gain a hedged track. Turn left, and follow this for 200 yards to a signpost on the right. Here, go down to cross a stile, and then walk forward alongside a stream.

In the far corner of the field, cross another stile and continue to follow the stream into the next field. Bear half-left across an undulating pasture, passing beneath power lines, and aiming for the far left corner. Just before reaching the corner, cross a stile on the left. Walk up the edge of the next field for a short distance to another stile, on the right.

Over the stile, go forward with a hedge on your right to locate another stile in a hedge corner. Keep on in the same direction. Walk up the edge of the next field, and the one after that, to another step-stile near the top edge of a broad row of trees. Over the stile, strike diagonally left, crossing the field towards a gate and stile in a distant fence.

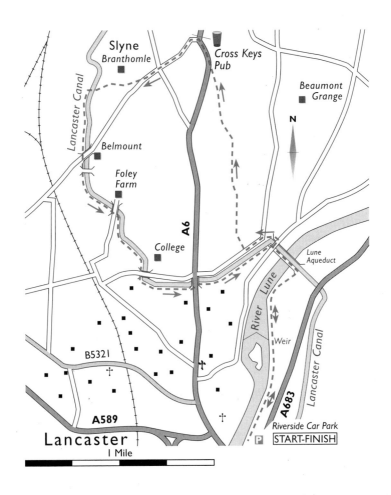

Just along this stretch there is a fine view of Morecambe Bay and the Lakeland Fells, from Black Combe near Millom in the west, to the southern fells around Coniston and the Langdale Pikes.

Go straight across the ensuing field. In the next, keep left to a stile, and then right along a fence to another stile near a metal gate. The map and route on the ground differ a little at this point. From the gate, go half-left across a sloping field to a metal kissing-gate in a hedge. From this, cross the final field to a gate, beyond which lies the A6 and the village of Slyne.

Tufted duck are a familiar year-round resident on Britain's waterways, building their nests in vegetation at the water's edge. Both male and female are recognisable by their yellow eyes and black-tipped grey bills.

Cross the road and walk up towards the Cross Keys pub. On reaching the pub, turn left along a road, noting the village stocks just on the left. Continue to a crossroads. Go forward into Hasty Brow Road, signposted for Torris-holme. Taking care against approaching traffic, walk along the road for a little over 100 yards. Branch right, down a narrow lane. As you reach the entrance to Brantholme, bear left through a gate. Now continue along a broad, hedgerowed track that runs on to reach and cross the Lancaster Canal.

As you cross the bridge, go through a gap on the right and walk down to the towpath. Turn right, passing back beneath the bridge. Now simply stroll along, all the way back to bridge 108, and the aqueduct. Turn down the steps to rejoin the riverside track, and return to the start of the walk.

Glasson Dock

> **Distance: 6¹/₂ miles (10.5 km)**
> **Time: 3 hours**
> **Terrain: Generally good paths, some road walking**
> **Start/Finish: Glasson Dock, grid ref GR445561**
> **Map: Explorer 296 (Lancaster, Morecambe & Fleetwood)**

It would be unthinkable in a book of walks based on Lancaster not to visit Glasson Dock, once an important Lune port, and today a busy marina. This is a hugely popular place at all times of year, and offers birdwatchers a chance of spotting regular migrants and the occasional rarity. Take binoculars.

Begin from the large car park opposite the Victoria Inn. Join the canal towpath, walking down it to Brows Bridge (no 8). Here, leave the towpath and go up to cross the bridge. Shortly, when the main road bends to the right, leave it by going forward into Jeremy Lane. Now, taking care against approaching traffic, simply follow Jeremy Lane through its various bends until it meets Moss Lane at a T-junction.

If you are interested in birdwatching, it is always useful to scan the flat fields either side of Jeremy Lane, as they often provide shelter and food for a wide range of species, and for brown hares.

When you reach Moss Lane, turn right for 300 yards. Leave the road by going left over a footbridge and into the corner of a field. Keep ahead alongside a hedge to a couple of stiles in a corner leading into a scrubby area adjoining fishing ponds. Keep on in the same direction towards Thursland Hill Farm. Go over a step-stile and immediately left through a gate. Follow the farm boundary round to the right. Now go straight on down the right-hand side of two pastures, later following a ditch. When the ditch changes direction, keep on, ahead, and cross the field to a gate.

From the gate, keep on to enter a hedged track. At the end of the track, turn left and walk out to a road. Turn right and walk down to the salt marsh at the edge of Cockerham Sands.

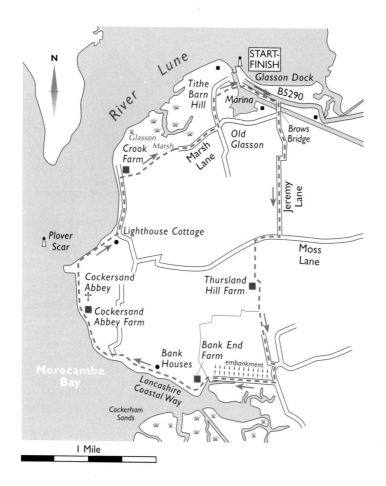

N

START-FINISH
Glasson Dock
B5290

River Lune

Tithe Barn Hill

Marina

Old Glasson

Brows Bridge

Glasson Crook Farm
Marsh
Marsh Lane

Jeremy Lane

Plover Scar

Lighthouse Cottage

Moss Lane

Cockersand Abbey
†

Thursland Hill Farm

Cockersand Abbey Farm

Bank Houses

Bank End Farm

embankment

Morecambe Bay

Lancashire Coastal Way

Cockerham Sands

1 Mile

Turn right, joining the Lancashire Coastal Way and following a road along the edge of the marsh, to Bank End Farm (an elevated embankment on the right gives a better view of the countryside if you're looking for birds, but this isn't a right of way). Pass to the left of Bank End Farm, and the caravan park beyond, to go forward along a raised embankment.

You meet a road again at the Cockerham Sands Country Park at Bank Houses. Beyond, you go through a gate and continue along a raised walkway. Head on to reach Cockersand Abbey.

19

Christ Church was built in 1840 by Lancaster architect Edmund Sharpe to serve the burgeoning port of Glasson Dock.

Continue to Lighthouse Cottage, which has an interesting lantern window facing out to sea. Carry on along a surfaced lane to Crook Farm. Here the Coastal Way turns inland and goes along a hedgerowed lane. The track later runs on alongside a hedge and then crosses a water channel at a gate. Continue across an open field. When you reach a line of old hawthorns, the track swings right to a metal gate at the end of Marsh Lane, near a caravan site.

Walk along Marsh Lane to a road junction. Go left, climbing gently to another road junction overlooking Glasson Marsh. Turn right, and walk down Tithe Barn Hill into Glasson Dock to complete the walk.

Galgate and Thurnham

> **Distance: 5¼ miles (8.5 km)**
> **Time: 2½ hours**
> **Terrain: Canal towpaths, tracks and farm fields**
> **Start/Finish: Galgate centre, grid ref 483553**
> **Map: Explorer 296 (Lancaster, Morecambe and Fleetwood)**

Begin from the centre of Galgate and walk south along the A6 to pass beneath the railway bridge. A short way further on, just after the Canalside Craft Centre (coffee shop here), turn right onto a signposted bridleway that soon crosses the Lancaster Canal. Over Galgate Bridge, turn left through a gate to join the towpath. Turn right, and walk past Galgate Marina.

After about 500 yards you meet a canal junction at the shapely Junction Bridge (bridge no 1). Turn right beneath the bridge, and pass the first of a number of locks along this Glasson branch of the Lancaster Canal, built in 1826. Then keep on along the towpath. This is a delightful stretch, and you often find swans, moorhen and the occasional kingfisher here.

Keep on until you reach bridge no 3. Go under it. A short way further on, go through a narrow stone stile on the right (near a gate). Turn immediately right and over the bridge. Cross a stile and start following a broad track. Eventually you pass to the right of Cock Hall Farm, beyond which you meet a road.

Turn right and go past the steepled church, built in 1847-8 for Miss Elizabeth Dalton of nearby Thurnham Hall. Keep ahead along the side of Thurnham Hall, now a country club. Walk along the track in front of the hall, passing to the left of converted barns to cross a car park. At the end of the car park, cross a stile on the left. In the ensuing field, bear half-right and then follow a hedgerow to a step-stile. Now bear right, back towards the canal, reaching it at Bailey Bridge. Cross the bridge, and either squeeze through a narrow stile on the left and descend rough steps (very slippery) to the canal towpath, or go through the gate and turn right down a ramp to a step-stile below leading onto the towpath. Turn right.

Continue along the canal as far as the Mill Inn. Leave the towpath here by branching right through a gate onto an access lane and walking out to

Primroses and violets are both familiar plants of woods, grassland and hedgerows, their flowers appearing between February and May.

Thurnham Mill Lane. Turn left to a T-junction, turn right over a bridge spanning the River Conder, and almost immediately bear right on a minor road. When the minor road is joined by another from the left, look for a step-stile (preceded by a stone squeeze-stile) in a corner, and cross this. Walk up-field, passing Webster's Farm.

The field edge continues to meet Crow Wood, where a stile in the corner on the right leads onto a narrow slab bridge spanning a stream. Cross this and turn left along the southern boundary of Crow Wood. Continue with a hedge on your left, across two fields to a squeeze stile at Parkside Farm.

Go ahead into the farmyard, but bear left and then right to pass through the yard and out the other side. Now keep on in the same direction, alongside a hedgerow until, at a metal field gate, you can cross a stile onto the other side.

Turn left to continue to the bottom edge of the field. There's a gate on the left and a step-stile ahead, across which you follow the left-hand edge of a small triangular field to an old metal stile. Over this, keep roughly the same

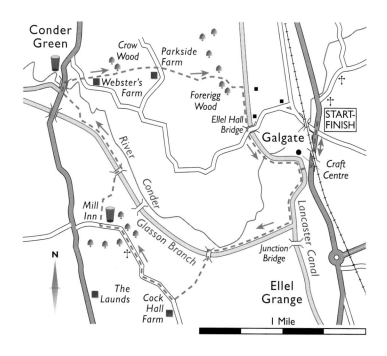

direction as you climb across the field, then descend to a stile leading into Forerigg Wood.

Go through the woodland. On the other side, bear right along the woodland boundary, passing a ladder-stile and gate. From here, bear half-left across a pasture to a step-stile leading onto the canal towpath. Turn right.

The first bridge you encounter is Ellel Hall Bridge, and if you leave the towpath here, you can turn along the road and follow it back to the centre of Galgate.

The preferred route continues to the next bridge, Galgate Bridge. Go beneath the bridge, turn right through a gate and right again to cross the bridge used at the start of the walk. Head out to meet the A6. Turn left to the centre of Galgate to complete the walk.

Lancaster: city and canal

> **Distance: 7 miles (11 km)**
> **Time: 3$\frac{1}{2}$ hours**
> **Terrain: canal towpath, a little road walking, and good tracks**
> **Start/Finish: Lancaster, Skerton Bridge, grid ref 479623**
> **Ordnance Survey map: Explorer 296 (Lancaster,**
> **Morecambe & Fleetwood)**

You should start or finish this walk with a tour of the city. It is dominated by two impressive monuments: the castle, still a prison, as it has been for centuries; and the Ashton Memorial above Williamson Park.

Begin from anywhere in the city by walking down to Skerton Bridge. Continue on a surfaced track down an avenue of trees in the River Lune Millennium Park, with the river itself just a short distance away. (The early

part of the walk is shared with Walk 5.) Continue easily to the Lune Aqueduct. Turn right onto a narrow path that leads to a flight of steps. Ascend here to reach the towpath.

Turn right alongside the canal, which in springtime is brightened by water lily and iris, and host to a good number of birds, occasionally including a darting kingfisher. Now, simply follow the towpath.

At Whitecross (bridge 100), just as you pass Lancaster's cathedral, leave the canal by ascending a ramp on the right. Turn left and cross the bridge. Descend on the other side to reach the Whitecross pub. Keep on along the towpath, soon passing the Water Witch Pub. Shortly after, the towpath transfers back to the opposite side of the canal. (You need to go down a narrow flight of steps adjacent to apartments to rejoin the towpath by turning right beneath the bridge.)

Continue until you pass bridge 95. The canal now has a road very closely on the right, as it bends gently to the left. A short way on, leave the towpath and go onto the road.

A short stretch up to and through the village of Aldcliffe now follows. Take care against approaching traffic here. As you reach the village, turn into the

Lancaster's Lune waterfront.

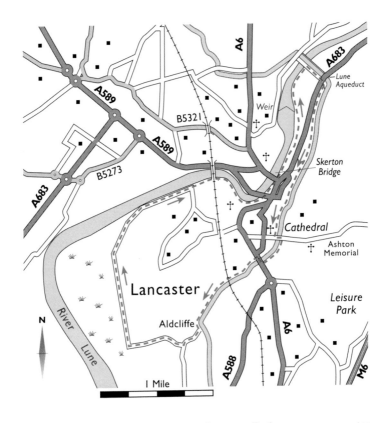

first lane on the right. Descend past housing, to walk along a narrow country lane to its end at a gravel turning area.

A clear, surfaced and very straight track now runs north from the gravel area. This can be followed all the way back to Lancaster, where you will arrive at St George's Quay, near the Millennium Bridge. Simply turn back up into town to complete the walk.

Littledale

> **Distance: 5 miles (8 km)**
> **Time: 2½ hours**
> **Terrain: often muddy paths and upland tracks; some road walking**
> **Start/Finish: Roadside parking near Cragg Farm, grid ref 546617**
> **Map: Explorer OL41 (Forest of Bowland & Ribblesdale)**

Littledale conceals itself among the folds of the hills south of Caton, and provides the opportunity for a little peaceful wandering through wooded cloughs and glens.

Set off from the roadside parking area, heading east, towards Cragg Farm. Close to the farm, cross a cattle grid to begin the long road descent into Littledale. At the bottom of the descent, a roadbridge takes you over Udale Beck. Go left to cross Foxdale Beck, then climb alongside beech woodland.

Continue to a road junction opposite New House Farm. Turn right along a lane for Littledale. Go past Crossgill Farm. At the entrance of a driveway to Littledale Hall, bear left. Climb gently past the Old Church House, the former church of St Anne, Littledale, built in 1750, but made redundant in 1978. Beyond the church, when the road bends sharply to the left, leave it on the apex, bearing right over a stile beside a gate. Go forward along a broad trail that heads into Littledale.

The track passes below a spruce plantation on the left, and leads on to another gate and stile, beyond which you continue beside a wall. Further on you pass yet another old church, a Free Church constructed in 1849 by the vicar of Cockerham, John Dodson, who also built the collection of buildings at Littledale Hall.

The track continues past the church, sandwiched between a wall and fence. As the wall bears to the right, above Littledale Hall, you keep left, heading towards Gill Plantation.

At this point, the route continues eastwards for another couple of miles before simply turning round and coming back on a lower path, little more than 100 yards below the place where you are now. Alas, no right-of-way

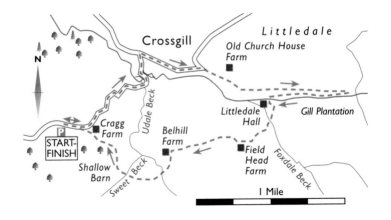

links the two paths, but that isn't a problem, because the onward walk is delightful, and the spot where you turn tail to come back would, on a fine summer's day, be ideal for a picnic.

So, just after passing below the plantation, the track runs to a gate. Here, keep to the right of the gate, walking alongside a wall and then a fence to a metal gate in a corner. This leads onto a narrow path between a fence and rhododendron. Keep alongside the fence and cross an in-flowing stream. Press on along the top edge of a wooded slope inhabited by pheasants.

The on-going path gradually descends away from the fence and moves down towards the dale bottom. At one point you cross a field track, with the return track just a few strides below you, but you must press on, crossing the track and climbing once more before resuming a more level course.

Eventually, the path descends towards a footbridge and ladder-stile. About fifty yards before reaching the footbridge, at the bottom of the descending path, you need to double back on yourself onto a lower path. Indistinct and intermittent for a time, this runs along the bottom of the slope you have just walked. It leads back to that field track you encountered earlier. Now join the track, going forward to a gate and stile at the foot of a wall, immediately adjoining the stream.

You part company with the stream for a short while at a gate and stile. From here, go forward towards Littledale Hall. Cross a bridge near the hall, and go left, ascending. Then turn right and left between farm buildings to find a metal gate. A track then leads on alongside Foxdale Beck to a footbridge.

28

The hare is a solitary mammal which favours open farmland.

Over the bridge, bear right onto an ascending path through woodland to a stile at the top boundary. Over the stile, bear right along a fence. Keep following the fence to a through-stile just before Field Head Farm. Cross to the right of the farm buildings to intercept the farm access track. Continue across the end of a small coppice and on to a cattle grid.

Just at this point, the observant will notice, just before the cattle grid, a through-stile on the left, and another stile a short distance further on, indicated by a yellow waymark. This is the line of the right-of-way here-abouts, which leads on to Bellhill Farm. However, if you go on to cross the cattle grid, another waymark clearly points out that use of the farm access is permitted. So walk along this, with a view in the far distance ahead of the Ashton Memorial in Lancaster.

Keep following the track as it descends to Bellhill Farm. Go across a cattle grid, and then turn left through an area where the farm buildings were converted to residential use early in 2006. Locate a gate to the right of the original Bellhill farmhouse. Descend briefly to a field gate and go down a track beside a fence. At the bottom, turn right at a waymark. Bear left to a ford and footbridge, where you meet Udale Beck again.

Over the bridge, walk up a stony track, but keep an eye open for a way-marked step-stile beside a metal gate on the right. Cross this to gain an ascending track around the edge of a small woodland, above which it continues alongside a fence. The track leads on to wooded Sweet Beck, set in a narrow ravine. Cross this and then walk up to nearby Skellow Barn.

Swing right past the barn, following a raised grassy track. Shortly walk alongside a wall, crossing a stile beside a gate. Go left at another gate onto a track rising to Cragg Farm, where the outward route is joined. Now simply turn left to return to the start.

Carnforth and the Keer

Distance: 6¼ miles (10 km)
Time: 2½ hours
Terrain: Generally good paths, canal towpath, a little road walking
Start/Finish: Carnforth town centre. GR497706.
Map: Explorer OL7 (The English Lakes: South-eastern area)

The renown of Carnforth tends to rest on the fact that the railway station was used in the film Brief Encounter, *but this modest town has much more going for it, not least a place on the coast overlooking Morecambe Bay, and easy access to the Lancaster Canal, one of the finest unsung stretches of waterside walking in Lancashire.*

Leave Carnforth along the road leading north from the railway station, for Warton and Millhead. On reaching Millhead, just after crossing the River Keer, turn right into a side street. Walk on below Carlisle Terrace to pass a bowling green and football pitch. At the end of the track, go through a kissing-gate, and half-left along a path for Warton. On the far side of the field, go through another gate and keep alongside a hedge. At the far end of the field, pass through another gate and

Canada geese can be seen on inland stretches of water such as Pine Lake.

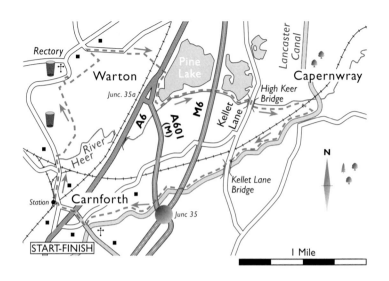

along a track between houses to an estate road. Turn right to come to the end of a cul-de-sac. Here, turn left onto a path that leads towards the main village road.

Turn right here, and walk past the Malt Shovel pub. A few strides further on, turn right through an archway to follow a path between houses to a step-stile. Go straight on across the end of a field to a gap-stile. Through this, turn right alongside a wall to a gap at a hedge corner. Through the gap, turn left. Go through another hedge gap. Keep on in the same direction to the field corner, where another stile leads onto an enclosed path at the rear of houses. When you intercept another path between houses, turn left. Follow this until you can move right to join Well Lane and continue up to a T-junction.

Just at the T-junction, rather than turn right and walk along a road with no footpath, take to a parallel road in front of houses. When the houses end, you emerge onto the road. Now take care against approaching traffic, and follow the road as far as a farm on the right. Leave the road by turning right onto a path for Pine Lake. The path descends as a broad track between hedges, continues beneath a railway line, and runs out to meet the A6.

Cross the A6 with care and go over an old metal stile opposite. Turn right along a path for High Keer Bridge, that passes around the edge of the Pine Lake holiday complex. The path emerges at the entrance to Pine Lake. Cross

31

to a continuing path opposite. Follow this until you meet the River Keer once more.

Turn left, now in company with the river, as you will be for some time. Heading upstream, keep going and you will pass below the M6. On the other side, keep alongside the Keer.

Keep following the river until you meet a road (Kellet Lane). Here is High Keer Bridge. Cross the bridge and immediately go left down steps into the corner of a pasture. Now resume the riverside course, crossing stiles, and eventually passing beneath a railway viaduct. Go across to the top left corner of the field beyond the viaduct, to locate a stile beside a gate.

Over the stile, cross left to a five-bar gate leading onto the canal towpath. Turn right and now simply follow the canal all the way back to Carnforth. Stay on the towpath until you reach bridge 128, which has an accompanying pedestrian bridge alongside it. Here, walk on to pass a children's play area. Leaving the towpath, take a path that curls back around the play area to pop out onto a road. Turn left and walk down to the centre of Carnforth. Cross the A6 at the traffic lights to complete the walk